Level 3 Diploma in Accounting
Accounts Preparation I

First Edition 2010
Third Edition 2012

ISBN 9781 4453 9472 5 (previous ISBN 9780 7517 9745 9)

British Library Cataloguing-in-Publication Data

A catalogue record for this book is available from the British Library

Published by

BPP Learning Media Ltd, BPP House, Aldine Place, London W12 8AA

www.bpp.com/learningmedia

Printed in the United Kingdom

Your learning materials, published by BPP Learning Media Ltd,
are printed on paper sourced from sustainable, managed forests.

Welcome to BPP Learning Media's AAT **Passcards for Accounts Preparation 1.**

- They **save you time**. Important topics are summarised for you.
- They incorporate **diagrams** to kick-start your memory.
- They follow the overall **structure** of the BPP Text, but BPP Learning Media's AAT **Passcards** are not just a condensed book. Each card has been separately designed for clear presentation. Topics are self contained and can be grasped visually.
- AAT **Passcards** are **just the right size** for pockets, briefcases and bags.
- AAT **Passcards focus on the assessment** you will be facing.
- AAT **Passcards focus on the essential points** that you need to know in the workplace, or when completing your assessment.

Run through the complete set of **Passcards** as often as you can during your final revision period. The day before the assessment, try to go through the **Passcards** again! You will then be well on your way to completing your assessment successfully.

Good luck!

		Page

1: Accounting principles

Topic List

Purpose of an accounting system

Primary documents and books of prime entry

Ledger accounts

Principles of double entry bookkeeping

The trial balance

This chapter covers the purpose of maintaining financial records and revises some topics that you should already be familiar with from your previous studies.

Purpose of an accounting system

To ensure that all transactions are correctly recorded and can be gathered together for a period in order to prepare a set of financial statements

- To ensure the business can keep track of all its assets and activities
- To facilitate the measurement of the business's performance
- To help obtain financing and other forms of credit
- To meet statutory requirements

The accounting system

For each transaction there will be a primary document which is entered in a book of prime entry as the primary record.

Transactions	*Primary document*	*Book of prime entry*
Cash sales	Receipt/till roll	Cash receipts book
Credit sales	Sales invoice	Sales day book
Sales returns	Credit note	Sales returns day book
Receipts from credit customers	Remittance advice note	Cash receipts book
Cash purchases	Cheque book stub/till receipt	Cash payments book
Credit purchases	Purchase invoice	Purchases day book
Purchases returns	Credit note from supplier	Purchases returns day book
Payments to credit suppliers	Cheque book stub/bank authorisation	Cash payments book
Cash payments	Petty cash voucher	Petty cash payments book
Wages and salaries	Payroll records	Journal

The totals and detail from each book of prime entry is transferred (posted) to the general ledger accounts using the principles of double entry bookkeeping.

General ledger (main or nominal ledger)

Contains a separate ledger account for each type of income, expense, asset, liability and capital of a business

Memorandum ledgers

Do not form part of the double entry bookkeeping system

Sales ledger

Contains a ledger account for each individual receivable showing the amount owed by the customer and how it is made up

Purchases ledger

Contains a ledger account for each individual payable showing the amount owed to the supplier and how it is made up

There are three main principles of double entry bookkeeping.

Dual effect on business

Each transaction has two effects on the business eg the business buys goods for resale with cash – goods have increased and cash has decreased

Separate entity concept

The owner of the business is a separate entity from the business

Accounting equation

The accounting equation will always balance

ASSETS – LIABILITIES = CAPITAL

1: Accounting principles

D	**DEBIT** Increases in	**C**	**CREDIT** Increases in
E	EXPENSES eg incur advertising costs	**L**	LIABILITIES eg buy goods on credit
A	ASSETS eg new office equipment	**I**	INCOME eg make a sale
D	DRAWINGS eg the owner takes cash for his own use	**C**	CAPITAL eg owner puts money into the business
	Decreases in liabilities, capital or income		Decreases in assets, drawings or expenses
	Left hand side		**Right hand side**

Every transaction has a debit and a credit.

If a business buys goods for resale with cash then:

DEBIT   Purchases
CREDIT   Cash

Cash sales result in:

DEBIT   Cash
CREDIT   Sales

Total debits = Total credits

Accounting equation

Assets = Liabilities + Capital

Profit = Income − Expenditure

This is an example of balancing a ledger account.

RECEIVABLES

	£		£
Sales	10,000	Cash	8,000
		Balance c/d	2,000
	10,000		10,000
Balance b/d	2,000		

At the end of an accounting period the closing balance is calculated on each ledger account.

- Total all debits and credits
- Debits exceed credits = debit balance
- Credits exceed debits = credit balance

The balances are collected in a trial balance. If the double entry is correct, total debit balances = total credit balances.

2: Accounting concepts

Topic List

Statement of financial position

Income statement

Accounting standards

Accounting concepts

This chapter looks at the content of the financial statements and the conceptual basis of accounts preparation.

Statement of financial position

Statement of financial position: a statement of the assets, liabilities and capital of a business at a given time

It is a 'snapshot' of the business on the last day of the period

Income statement

Income statement: a statement of revenue earned and costs incurred in earning it

The income statement usually highlights **gross profit** and **profit for the period**.

The **top part** shows the gross profit for the period:

Gross profit = Sales − Cost of goods sold

Profit for the period is then calculated:

Profit for the period = Gross profit − Other expenses

PROFORMA STATEMENT OF FINANCIAL POSITION AT 31 MARCH 20XX

	£	£
Non-current assets		X
Current assets		
Inventory	X	
Receivables	X	
Cash at bank and in hand	X	
	A	
Current liabilities		
Payables	X	
Bank overdraft	X	
	B	
Net current assets (A – B)		X
Non-current liabilities		(X)
Net assets		C
Capital		
Proprietor's capital		X
Retained profits (including previous and current period profits)		X
		C

The income statement

Summarises all income and expenditure which has arisen during a trading period.

Gross profit = sales − cost of sales

Profit for the period = gross profit − expenses

PROFORMA INCOME STATEMENT
FOR THE PERIOD ENDED 31 MARCH 20XX

	£	£
Sales revenue		X
Less: cost of sales		
Opening inventory	X	
Purchases	X	
Less: closing inventory	(X)	
		(X)
Gross profit		X
Less expenses		
Rent	X	
Wages	X	
Bank charges	X	
Insurance	X	
Depreciation	X	
Repairs and maintenance	X	
Irrecoverable debt expense	X	
		(X)
Profit for the period		X

Development of accounting standards

Accounting standards: a set of rules which prescribe the methods by which financial statements should be prepared and presented

Relevant standards for AP1

| IAS 16 | Property, plant and equipment (FRS 15 Tangible fixed assets) |
| IAS 2 | Inventories, (SSAP 9 Stocks and long-term contracts) |

UK standards

SSAPs – Statements of Standard Accounting Practice

FRSs – Financial Reporting Standards

Worldwide standards

IASs – International Accounting Standards

IFRSs – International Financial Reporting Standards

The UK and worldwide standards are broadly similar with some differences in terminology. AAT assessments are using IFRS terminology from January 2012.

2: Accounting concepts

What are accounting concepts?

Accounting concepts are the **assumptions** underlying the financial statements. The most important accounting concepts are **going concern** and **accruals** (or matching).

Accruals (matching)

Income must be matched against the costs incurred in earning it.

Income or expense in income statement is amount earned or incurred during the accounting period – not the cash received or paid.

Going concern

Assumes that the business will continue to operate into the foreseeable future at its current level of activity.

Other concepts

Prudence

Where there is uncertainty, amounts included in the accounts must be prudent ie a degree of caution is required to ensure:

- Assets/income are not overstated
- Liability/expenses are not understated
- Prudence means the most cautious amount is used
- Where a loss is foreseen it should be accounted for using an estimate based on the best information available
- Profit should not be accounted for until it is realised

Consistency

- To make financial statements more useful and comparable
- The same presentation and classification should be applied from one period to another

Materiality

Concerns the accounting treatment of small items

- In practice the rules which underlie the preparation of accounts do not need to apply to non-material items

    (eg charging small capital items to the income statement rather than treating as non-current assets)

- What is a material amount depends on the size of the business

3: Non-current assets

Topic List

Capital v revenue

Purchases

Non-current assets register

Depreciation

Disposals

Reconciliation

This is a very important chapter. It covers accounting for non-current assets which will be tested in the first part of the assessment.

Non-current assets: the basics

Non-current asset: acquired and retained within the business with a view to earning profits, normally used over more than one accounting period

Examples

- Plant and machinery eg machine used in manufacturing
- Motor vehicles eg delivery vans, managers' cars
- Land and buildings eg building from which business operates
- Furniture and fittings
- Computer equipment

Capital expenditure

Cost of buying non-current assets and getting them into operation, eg purchase price, delivery and installation costs, alterations and professional fees.

Revenue expenditure

All other expenditure of the business other than purchase of non-current assets eg decorating, repairs and maintenance costs.

Recording capital purchases

The purchase may be recorded in the **cash book** or in the **purchases day book**.

However, the purchase is most likely to be recorded with a **journal**.

Journal 2

13 Sept XX	DEBIT	Plant & machinery	£14,000
	DEBIT	VAT at 20%	£2,800
	CREDIT	Cash	£16,800

Being cash purchase of printing machine

Journal 1

| 13 Sept XX | DEBIT | Motor vehicles a/c | £13,200 |
| | CREDIT | Purchases ledger control a/c | £13,200 |

Being purchase of Peugeot 206 LM23 OLE on credit

Alert: VAT on cars that have some private usage is not recoverable and is therefore capitalised as part of the cost of the car

Assets made by the business

A business may construct or install a non-current asset for its own use, using its own labour and materials

→

Cost of the non-current asset includes the wages cost of the employees and any materials that have been used

↓

Journal

13 Sept XX DEBIT Non-current assets £15,000
CREDIT Wages £5,000
CREDIT Purchases £10,000

Being installation of a new specialised machine using own labour and purchased materials.

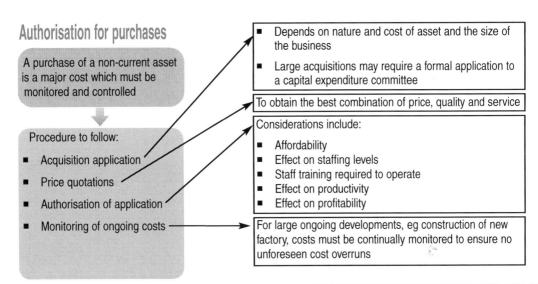

Authorisation for purchases

A purchase of a non-current asset is a major cost which must be monitored and controlled

Procedure to follow:

- Acquisition application
- Price quotations
- Authorisation of application
- Monitoring of ongoing costs

- Depends on nature and cost of asset and the size of the business
- Large acquisitions may require a formal application to a capital expenditure committee

To obtain the best combination of price, quality and service

Considerations include:

- Affordability
- Effect on staffing levels
- Staff training required to operate
- Effect on productivity
- Effect on profitability

For large ongoing developments, eg construction of new factory, costs must be continually monitored to ensure no unforeseen cost overruns

Funding

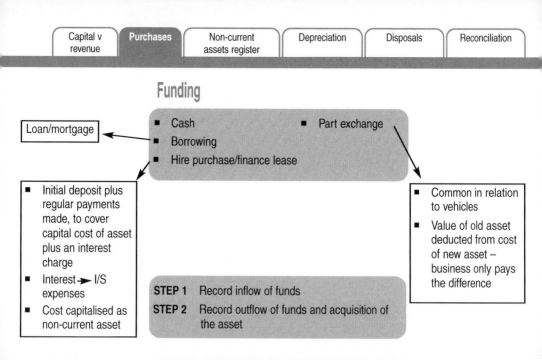

Cash
Borrowing
Hire purchase/finance lease
Part exchange

Loan/mortgage

- Initial deposit plus regular payments made, to cover capital cost of asset plus an interest charge
- Interest → I/S expenses
- Cost capitalised as non-current asset

- Common in relation to vehicles
- Value of old asset deducted from cost of new asset – business only pays the difference

STEP 1 Record inflow of funds
STEP 2 Record outflow of funds and acquisition of the asset

Non-current assets register

Non-current assets register: listing of all assets owned by the organisation.

- Not part of the double entry
- An internal control

Likely details:

- Description and location of asset
- Purchase date and supplier
- Cost
- Depreciation method and estimated useful life
- Accumulated depreciation b/d and c/d
- Disposal date and proceeds
- Profit/loss on disposal

Depreciation

Depreciation: the measure of the cost of the economic benefits of the asset that have been consumed during the period

Depreciation is charged to allocate a fair proportion of the non-current asset's cost to the period benefiting from its use.

$$\boxed{\text{Carrying amount of asset}} = \boxed{\text{Cost}} - \boxed{\text{Accumulated depreciation}}$$

DEBIT ⟶ Income statement ⟶ Depreciation charge for the year
CREDIT ⟶ Statement of financial position ⟶ Accumulated depreciation

Depreciation policies

- State the method used for each type of non-current asset
- Consistency concept demands same method is used each year

Methods of depreciation

Straight line

Cost of asset – residual value
Expected useful life of asset

The depreciation charge is the same year on year.

Reducing balance

The carrying amount of the asset × fixed % rate.

The depreciation charge is higher in the first years of the asset's life.

Expected scrap value at end of useful life

Time period estimated that asset will be used in the business

Alert. Make sure that you learn both methods of depreciation and make sure that you apply the correct method.

Recording depreciation in the accounts

1 Bring the credit balance of the accumulated depreciation account down.

2 Depreciation charge for the year:

DEBIT Depreciation expense (I/S)
CREDIT Accumulated depreciation a/c (SFP)

3 Non-current asset account is unchanged, showing the cost of the non-current asset.

Carrying amount = Non-current asset cost less accumulated depreciation

Disposing of non-current assets

	£	£
Sales proceeds		X
Less cost of making the sale		(X)
Net sale proceeds		X
Cost of non-current asset	X	
Less accumulated depreciation	(X)	
Carrying amount		(X)
Profit/(loss) on disposal		X/(X)

1 Calculate the profit/loss on disposal

2 The following must appear in the disposals account:

    (a) Original cost of the asset (DR)

    (b) Accumulated depreciation (CR)

    (c) Net sales proceeds (CR)

3 Ledger accounting entries:

(a) DEBIT   Disposals account
CREDIT   Non-current asset account
with cost of asset

(b) DEBIT   Accumulated depreciation a/c
CREDIT   Disposals account
with accumulated dep'n

(c) DEBIT   Cash/bank account
CREDIT   Disposals account
with proceeds of asset sale

4 The balance on the disposal account is the profit/loss on disposal which is recorded in the income statement ledger account.

DISPOSALS ACCOUNT			
	£		£
Non-current asset a/c	200	Accumulated depn a/c	100
Income statement (profit)	30	Cash a/c	130
	230		230

Alert. Disposals are a key area. Make sure you can post the ledger entries correctly.

Part exchange

The part exchange allowance is part of the cost of the new asset and the disposal proceeds of the old asset.

The journals required are:

1 DEBIT   New non-current asset account
    CREDIT   Disposal account
    with the part exchange allowance

2 DEBIT   New non-current asset account
    CREDIT   Cash/bank account
    with the balance paid for the new asset

Disposals, like acquisitions, need to be authorised.

Reconciling physical assets, ledger accounts and register

The non-current assets register must reconcile (agree) with both the general ledger and the assets themselves.

Physical checks

- Check asset in register still exists in the business
- Check that each asset in the business is recorded in the register

Discrepancies

Discrepancies have to be investigated.

- Asset in business not in register → when asset purchased no entries put in register
- Entries in register not up to date, eg depreciation charge not entered each year
- Asset in register but no physical asset → asset sold/scrapped/stolen and not recorded

4: Accruals and prepayments

You've met the concept of accruals before – this chapter tells you how to deal with them in practice.

Accrued of expenses

Where expenses have been incurred but not invoiced/paid for at the end of the accounting period

Expense incurred – no invoice yet

Part relating to current accounting period is an accrual (a liability in the SFP).

We **debit** the expense account with the expense (as an 'accrual c/d') and **credit** it with the liability (as an 'accrual b/d').

Example

A business has a debit balance of £1,200 on its gas account for the year to 31 March 20X4. On 3 June 20X4 it receives a bill for £900 for the 3 months to 31 May 20X4. £900 × 1/3 = accrual of £300.

GAS ACCOUNT

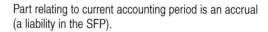

		£			£
31.3.X4	Bal b/d	1,200	31.3.X4	IS a/c	1,500
31.3.X4	Accrual c/d	300			
		1,500			1,500
			1.4.X4	Accrual b/d	300

Prepayment of expenses

> Where an expense has been paid in the accounting period, but it relates to the following accounting period

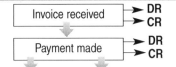

| Invoice received | **DR** Expense account
 CR PLCA account |
| Payment made | **DR** PLCA account
 CR Cash/bank account |

Expense stays in IS ← Part that relates to current accounting period

Part that relates to later accounting period → Prepayment. An asset in the SFP, not charged as an expense in the IS

We **credit** the expense account with the accounts prepaid (as 'prepayment c/d'), thereby reducing the expense, and **debit** it with the asset (as 'prepayment b/d').

Example

A business pays an insurance premium of £1,500 for the year to 31 March 20X5 on 1 April 20X4. The business's year end is 31 December. £1,500 × 3/12 = prepayment of £375

INSURANCE a/c

	£		£
01.04.X4 Bank	1,500	31.12.X4 IS	1,125
		31.12.X4 Prepayment c/d	375
	1,500		1,500
1.1.X5 Prepayment b/d	375		

Prepayments of income

Where sundry income (eg rent) is received for a period extending beyond the end of the accounting period.

Proportion of income related to future periods is shown in the statement of financial position as a current liability, prepaid income (income received in advance).

Year end journal:

DR Income account ('prepaid income c/d')

CR Income account ('prepaid income b/d') = liability

Accruals of income

Where sundry income (eg interest receivable, commissions) has been earned but not received.

Income earned in accounting period is credited to the IS and a corresponding asset (accrued income) is recognised in the SFP.

Year end journal:

DR Income account ('accrued income b/d') = asset

CR Income account ('accrued income c/d') = increase in income

Recording depreciation in the accounts

1 Bring the credit balance of the accumulated depreciation account down.

2 Depreciation charge for the year:

DEBIT   Depreciation expense (I/S)
CREDIT   Accumulated depreciation a/c (SFP)

3 Non-current asset account is unchanged, showing the cost of the non-current asset.

> Carrying amount = Non-current asset cost less accumulated depreciation

3 Ledger accounting entries:

(a) DEBIT Disposals account
    CREDIT Non-current asset account
    with cost of asset

(b) DEBIT Accumulated depreciation a/c
    CREDIT Disposals account
    with accumulated dep'n

(c) DEBIT Cash/bank account
    CREDIT Disposals account
    with proceeds of asset sale

4 The balance on the disposal account is the profit/loss on disposal which is recorded in the income statement ledger account.

DISPOSALS ACCOUNT			
	£		£
Non-current asset a/c	200	Accumulated depn a/c	100
Income statement (profit)	30	Cash a/c	130
	230		230

Alert. Disposals are a key area. Make sure you can post the ledger entries correctly.

Reconciling physical assets, ledger accounts and register

The non-current assets register must reconcile (agree) with both the general ledger and the assets themselves.

Physical checks

- Check asset in register still exists in the business
- Check that each asset in the business is recorded in the register

Discrepancies

Discrepancies have to be investigated.

- Asset in business not in register ← when asset purchased no entries put in register
- Entries in register not up to date, eg depreciation charge not entered each year
- Asset in register but no physical asset ← asset sold/scrapped/stolen and not recorded

Accrued of expenses

Where expenses have been incurred but not invoiced/paid for at the end of the accounting period

Expense incurred – no invoice yet

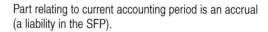

Part relating to current accounting period is an accrual (a liability in the SFP).

We **debit** the expense account with the expense (as an 'accrual c/d') and **credit** it with the liability (as an 'accrual b/d').

Example

A business has a debit balance of £1,200 on its gas account for the year to 31 March 20X4. On 3 June 20X4 it receives a bill for £900 for the 3 months to 31 May 20X4. £900 × 1/3 = accrual of £300.

GAS ACCOUNT

		£			£
31.3.X4	Bal b/d	1,200	31.3.X4	IS a/c	1,500
31.3.X4	Accrual c/d	300			
		1,500			1,500
			1.4.X4	Accrual b/d	300

Accrued
expenses

**Prepayment of
expenses**

Accruals and
prepayments of income

Example

A business pays an insurance premium of £1,500
for the year to 31 March 20X5 on 1 April 20X4. The
business's year end is 31 December. £1,500 × 3/12
= prepayment of £375

INSURANCE a/c

	£		£
01.04.X4 Bank	1,500	31.12.X4 IS	1,125
		31.12.X4 Prepayment c/d	375
	1,500		1,500
1.1.X5 Prepayment b/d	375		

5: Inventory

This is an important chapter. It covers inventory, which is a key figure in both the income statement and the statement of financial position.

Overview of inventory

Under the accruals concept only the cost of goods sold in the period should be charged to the income statement. An adjustment is made at the year end to reflect the value in inventory.

End of year procedures

- Physically count the inventory
- Value the inventory
- Adjust the ledger accounts to reflect the value of closing inventory

Physical count of inventory

Physical count

At the end of the accounting period each item of inventory is physically counted and listed.

Stores records

Records quantity purchased for each delivery, quantity issued for sale/processing and the quantity on hand

Reconciliation

Quantity counted is compared to the stores records. All discrepancies must be investigated

- Errors in recording deliveries/issues
- Stolen items

Value of closing inventory

Quantity of inventory $\times$ Value per item $=$ Value of inventory

Rule for valuing inventory (IAS 2 & SSAP 9)

Inventory is valued at the **lower** of:
- Cost and
- Net realisable value

Cost

- IAS 2 – all costs of purchase, costs of conversion and other costs incurred in bringing the items to their present location and condition
- SSAP 9 – cost of getting the inventory into its current position (includes delivery charges)

Net realisable value (NRV)

The expected selling price of the inventory, less any further costs to be incurred such as selling or distribution costs

Methods of determining cost

Where deliveries and issues of inventory are made on a regular basis, it is impossible, in practice, to determine precisely which items have been sold and which remain in inventory at the year end. The cost of inventory is therefore determined using one of the following methods.

First in, First out (FIFO)

Assumes:
- Items issued/sold are the earliest purchases
- Inventory comprises the most recent purchases

Last in, First out (LIFO)

Assumes:
- Items issued/sold are the most recent purchases
- Inventory comprises the earliest purchases
- NB LIFO is not permitted under IAS 2

Weighted average cost (AVCO)

- After each purchase a weighted average cost per item is calculated:

$$\frac{\text{total cost of items held}}{\text{number of units held}}$$

- Inventory is valued at the average cost at the end of the year

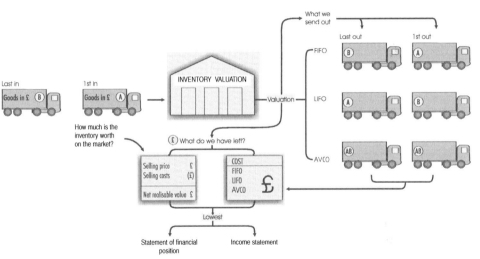

Entries during the year

During the year, purchases are recorded by the following entry:

DEBIT   Purchases
CREDIT   Purchases ledger control a/c

No entries are made in the inventory account

Calculation of cost of sales

	£
Opening inventory	X
Plus purchases	X
Less: Closing inventory	(X)
Cost of sales	X

Entries at the year end

Closing inventory

When the year end inventory has been counted and valued the following entries are made:

DEBIT   Inventory account – statement of financial position
CREDIT   Inventory account – income statement

Purchases

The balance on purchases account is cleared to the income statement ledger account

Opening inventory

The opening inventory figure remains in the accounts as the balance brought down on the inventory account from the previous year. The following entries are made to clear this figure:

DEBIT   Inventory account – income statement
CREDIT   Inventory account – statement of financial position

6: Irrecoverable debts and doubtful debts

Irrecoverable debts and doubtful debts are considered at the end of the accounting period. Irrecoverable debts may require writing out of the accounts and doubtful debts should have an allowance made against them.

Irrecoverable debts and doubtful debts

Under the prudence concept a receivable (debtor) should only be classed as an asset if it is recoverable.

Irrecoverable debts

If definitely irrecoverable, it should be written off as an irrecoverable debts expense.

DEBIT   Irrecoverable debts expense (IS)
CREDIT Sales ledger control a/c (SFP)

The customer's individual account in the sales ledger is also credited to remove the debt.

Doubtful debts

If uncertainty exists as to the recoverability of the debt, prudence dictates that an allowance for doubtful debts should be set up. This allowance is offset against the receivables balance in the statement of financial position.

DEBIT   Allowance for doubtful debts adjustment expense (IS)
CREDIT Allowance for doubtful debts a/c (SFP)

The allowance for doubtful debts can either be specific, against a particular receivable, or general, against a proportion of all receivables that are not specifically allowed for.

When calculating a general allowance for doubtful debts to be made, the following order applies:

	£
Receivables balance per SLCA	X
Less: irrecoverable debts written off	(X)
debts with a specific allowance	(X)
Balance on which general allowance is calculated	X

Note. Only the **movement** in the allowance (including both general and specific amount) needs to be accounted for.

	£
Allowance required at year end	X
Existing allowance (general and specific)	(X)
Increase/(decrease) required	X/(X)

Accounting entries

		DR	CR
(1)	Write off irrecoverable debts	Irrecoverable debt expense (IS)	Sales ledger control (SFP)
(2)	Set up allowance	Allowance for doubtful debts adjustment a/c (IS)	Allowance for doubtful debts (SFP)
(3)	Increase allowance	Allowance for doubtful debts adjustment a/c (IS)	Allowance for doubtful debts (SFP)
(4)	Reduce allowance	Allowance for doubtful debts (SFP)	Allowance for doubtful debts adjustment a/c (IS)

Subsequent recovery of debts written off

If a debt is recovered, having previously been written off
in a previous period as irrecoverable, then:

DEBIT   Cash/Bank
CREDIT   Irrecoverable debts expense a/c

7: Bank reconciliations

Topic List

Checking the bank statement to the cash book

Preparing the bank reconciliation

This is an important chapter. The bank reconciliation is a key means of control of one of business's key assets, cash held at the bank. It is very likely that this topic will be tested in your assessment.

Purpose of bank reconciliations

- To identify errors – made either by the business in writing up the books or by the bank in maintaining the account
- To identify omissions eg bank charges, dishonoured cheques, and unpresented cheques sent to suppliers
- To verify the accuracy of the bank balance in the year end financial statements

Checking the bank statement to the cash book

STEP 1 Tick all of the receipts on the bank statement to the entries in the bank receipts column of the cash book

STEP 2 Tick all of the payments on the bank statement to the entries in the bank payments column of the cash book

STEP 3 Check any unticked items on the bank statement to ensure the bank has not made a mistake

STEP 4 Make any necessary adjustments to the general ledger to record any legitimate unticked items on the bank statement

Examples of cash book adjustments

- Bank giro credit from a customer not recorded in the cash book
- Bank charges not entered in the cash book
- The amount of a cheque incorrectly recorded in the cash book
- A cheque from a customer dishonoured by the bank

Alert! Remember that the bank statement and the cash book are mirror images of each other, ie a debit entry in the cash book is a credit on the bank statement

- After correcting the cash book for legitimate differences from the bank statement, we can calculate the correct balance for the bank account in the cash book

- We can now produce the bank reconciliation statement – the cash book balance is unlikely to agree to the bank statement because of **timing differences**

Bank reconciliation statement

	£
Balance per bank statement	X
Plus: Outstanding lodgements	X
Less: Unpresented cheques	(X)
Balance as per corrected cash book	X

Timing differences

Outstanding lodgements
Cash/cheques from customers paid into the bank and recorded in the cash book, which do not appear on the bank statement due to the delay caused by the clearing system

Unpresented cheques
Cheques to suppliers entered in the cash book, which do not appear on the bank statement as they have not yet been either banked by the supplier or cleared by the bank

8: Control account reconciliations

Topic List

Accounting for sales on credit

Sales ledger control account

Accounting for purchases on credit

Purchases ledger control account

Control account reconciliations

In this chapter we consider the reconciliations that are prepared for the sales ledger and purchases ledger control accounts with the sales and purchases ledgers respectively. You must be able to perform the reconciliations and process any adjustments required.

Basic accounting system for sales on credit

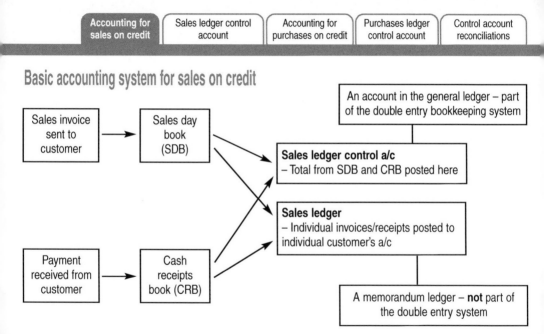

Sales ledger control account

As well as the basic entries for invoices and cash, the control account will contain other entries for items such as discounts allowed, debts written off, etc.

Sales ledger control account (SLCA)

	£		£
Balance b/d	X	Sales returns	X
Credit sales	X	Receipts from customers	X
Dishonoured cheques	X	Discounts allowed	X
		Irrecoverable debts written off	X
		Contra entry with PLCA	X
		Balance c/d	X
	$\overline{\underline{X}}$		$\overline{\underline{X}}$
Balance b/d	X		

Source
- Dishonoured cheques – bank returns customer's cheque unpaid – Debit SLCA, Credit Bank
- Sales returns – from sales returns day book
- Discounts allowed – from memorandum discounts allowed column in cash receipts book
- Contra entry (set off) – an amount owing by a customer which is set off against the amount owed by the business to them as a supplier. The other side of the entry is in the purchases ledger control account.

Basic accounting system for purchases on credit

```
┌─────────────────┐      ┌──────────────┐
│ Purchase        │      │ Purchases    │
│ invoice         │ ───▶ │ day book     │
│ received from   │      │ (PDB)        │
│ supplier        │      │              │
└─────────────────┘      └──────────────┘

┌─────────────────┐      ┌──────────────┐
│ Payment         │      │ Cash         │
│ made to         │ ───▶ │ payments     │
│ supplier        │      │ book (CPB)   │
└─────────────────┘      └──────────────┘
```

An account in the general ledger – part of the double entry bookkeeping system

Purchases ledger control a/c
– Totals from PDB and CPB posted

Purchases ledger
– Individual invoices/payments posted to individual supplier's a/c

A memorandum ledger – **not** part of the double entry system

Purchases ledger control account

As well as the basic entries for invoices and cash the control account will contain other entries for items such as discounts received, purchases returned, etc.

Purchases ledger control account (PLCA)

	£		£
Purchases returns	X	Balance b/d	X
Payments to suppliers	X	Credit purchases	X
Discounts received	X		
Contra entry with SLCA	X		
Balance c/d	X		
	X		X
		Balance b/d	X

Source

- Purchases returns – from purchases returns day book
- Discounts received – from memorandum discounts received column in cash payments book
- Contra entry (set off) – an amount owed to a supplier which is set off against the amount owed by the supplier as a credit customer. The other side of the entry is in the sales ledger control account

Balance on the control account   Should =   Total of balances in the memorandum ledger

SLCA = Receivables in statement of financial position

PLCA – Payables in statement of financial position

Purpose of control account reconciliation

- To **verify the accuracy** of the receivables and payables figures in the year end financial statements

- To identify **errors and omissions** made by the business in writing up the books

The reconciliation

- A comparison of the balance on the control account with the total of the list of the balances from the memorandum ledger, to check for errors and omissions

- All errors and omissions must be noted and appropriate adjustments made to the accounts via the journal

Examples of errors affecting the control account
■ Books of prime entry under- or over-cast
■ Postings from books of prime entry made to wrong side of control account
■ Discounts recorded in the cash book incorrectly treated in the control account
■ Irrecoverable debts/contras not entered in the control account

Examples of errors affecting the memorandum ledger
■ Transaction in book of prime entry entered in wrong account
■ Postings from books of prime entry made to wrong side of the memorandum ledger
■ Entry from books of prime entry posted as wrong amount in the memorandum ledger

Example of error	*Adjustment required to control a/c or memorandum ledger*
Page of cash receipts book undercast by £500	Cr SLCA £500
Irrecoverable debt of £800 written off in customer account but not in SLCA	Cr SLCA £800
Cash receipt entered into customer's account as £150 instead of £510	Cr Sales ledger £360
Purchases day book overcast by £1,000	Dr PLCA £1,000
Purchase invoice entered into supplier's account as £450 instead of £540	Cr Purchases ledger £90
Total of discounts received in cash book of £850 credited to the PLCA	Dr PLCA £1,700 (£850 x 2)

9: The trial balance, errors and the suspense account

Topic List

The trial balance

Types of error

Adjustments

In this chapter we revise the types of error that may occur in accounts and whether these cause a suspense account to be created in the trial balance. We also look at clearing the suspense account and preparing a trial balance. Section two of the assessment will include tasks testing the preparation of a trial balance and the correction of errors in the trial balance.

Trial balance

A **trial balance** is a list of ledger balances shown in debit and credit columns.

The debits should equal the credits.

If the trial balance does not balance, you need to set up a suspense account.

Suspense account

This is a **temporary** account set up to make the trial balance balance. Errors need to be found and corrected, clearing the suspense account, before the financial statements are prepared.

Errors resulting on an imbalance in the trial balance (TB)

- One-sided entry
- Entry duplicated on one side, nothing on the other
- Unequal entries eg transposition error
- Balance incorrectly transferred to TB
- Balance omitted from the TB

→

- Result in the creation of a suspense account on the TB
- Correction of the errors will clear the suspense account

Type of error	Adjustment required
One-sided entry eg debit made in ledger but not the credit entry	Make the missing entry (credit) and post the other side (debit) to the suspense account (a/c)
Entry duplicated on one side, nothing on the other	Post the a/c that was posted on the wrong side with twice the amount and post the other side to the suspense a/c
Unequal entries eg £10 debited to purchases (correct amount £100), £100 credited to cash	In the a/c with the wrong posting, post an amount to correct it and post the other side to the suspense a/c. eg DR Purchases £90, CR Suspense a/c £90
Balance incorrectly transferred to TB eg Bank debit balance of £10,000 written into TB as £1,000 debit	In the a/c with the wrong balance, post an amount to correct the balance and post the other side to the suspense a/c. eg DR Bank £9,000, CR Suspense a/c £9,000
Balance omission	Enter the missing balance and post the amount on the other side in the suspense a/c

Journal

The journal records transactions **not covered by other books of original entry**.

Journals can be used to correct errors. The error **must** have a **debit equal** in value **to the credit**.

The format of a journal entry is:

Date	Reference	£	£
	Account to be debited	X	
	Account to be credited		X

Narrative to explain the transaction

Alert. You may be asked for the journal entry of a transaction in an assessment.

Year end adjustments

Journals are also used to process year end adjustments such as

- Depreciation charge
- Accruals and prepayments
- Irrecoverable debts and doubtful debts
- Opening and closing inventory figures

- **Balance ledger accounts:** once all the entries to correct errors and process other year end adjustments have been made, the ledger accounts are balanced to give amended closing balances.

- **Closing off the ledger accounts:**

  1 Income and expenses ledger accounts – the balances are cleared to the Income Statement Ledger account

  2 Asset, liability and capital ledger accounts – the closing balances on the accounts become the opening balances of the following year

A new trial balance is drawn up from the amended balances

SALES

	£		£
IS ledger a/c	10,000	Bal b/d	10,000

There is no opening balance at the beginning of the next year

PURCHASES LEDGER CONTROL a/c

	£		£
Balance c/d	8,150	Balance b/d	8,000
		Journal	150
	8,150		8,150
		Bal b/d	8,150

The closing balance of £8,150 becomes the opening balance for the following year

10: The extended trial balance

You will usually be given tasks involving an extended trial balance (ETB) in your assessment. You must understand the layout of the ETB, know how to process adjustments through the ETB and then extend each line in the appropriate income statement or statement of financial position column.

Extended trial balance (ETB): a technique that allows the initial trial balance to be adjusted for any errors or year end adjustments; it is then used as the basis for the preparation of the financial statements

The ETB headings are:

Ledger account	Ledger balance		Adjustments		Income statement		Statement of financial position	
	DR £	CR £	DR £	CR £	DR £	CR £	DR £	CR £

Preparing the ETB

1 Enter each ledger a/c balance as either a debit or credit in the ledger balance column. If debits don't equal credits, check the additions are correct, then insert a suspense account.

2 If there is a suspense account deal with the errors that have caused this. Enter the adjustments in the Adjustments columns. Check that the suspense a/c has been cleared by your adjustments.

3 Make any year end adjustments:
- accruals and prepayments
- adjustments to inventory figures (debit SFP with closing inventory, credit IS a/c with closing inventory)
- other adjustments (eg depreciation and irrecoverable debts)

You may need to enter some new account lines in the ETB.

4 Add the adjustments columns. Check the entries are correct and debits equal credits.

5 Add the figures across each line of the ETB and record total in IS or SFP as appropriate.

6 Add the income statement debits and credits to find the profit or loss for the year.

Take the profit or loss for the period to the statement of financial position columns:

- Profit = DEBIT IS = CREDIT SFP
- Loss = CREDIT IS = DEBIT SFP

7 Add up the debits and credits in the statement of financial position and ensure they are equal.

Alert! Remember	Income statement	–	Income
		–	Expenses
	Statement of financial position	–	Assets
		–	Liabilities
		–	Capital
	Opening inventory is a debit to the income statement (IS)		

Notes